N E W Y O R K

RICHARD RAMBECK

THE HISTORY OF THE
YANKEES

CREATIVE EDUCATION

Published by Creative Education
123 South Broad Street, Mankato, Minnesota 56001
Creative Education is an imprint of The Creative Company

Designed by Rita Marshall
Editorial assistance by Rosemary Wallner & John Nichols

Photos by: Corbis-Bettmann, Focus on Sports, Fotosport, SportsChrome.

Library of Congress Cataloging-in-Publication Data

Rambeck, Richard.
The History of the New York Yankees / by Richard Rambeck.
p. cm. — (Baseball)
Summary: Highlights the key personalities and memorable games in the
history of the team that has won 23 World Series titles and 34 American
League pennants.
ISBN: 0-88682-918-6

1. New York Yankees (Baseball team)—History—Juvenile literature.
[1. New York Yankees (Baseball team)—History. 2. Baseball—History.]
I. Title. II. Series: Baseball (Mankato, Minn.)

GV875.N4R186   1999
796.357'64'397471—dc21   97-14581

First edition

9 8 7 6 5 4 3 2 1

Known as the "Big Apple," New York City has more than twice the population of any other United States metropolis. Huge buildings, home to many business headquarters, tower over the city's downtown core.

But New York isn't all business. The largest city in the U.S. also has a grand sports tradition, one that includes the most successful professional team in the history of U.S. sports—baseball's New York Yankees. No American professional team has won as many championships as the Yankees, who have claimed 23 World Series titles. The team has also won an unbelievable 34 American League pennants. In

"The House That Ruth Built," Yankee Stadium.   5

addition, the New York club is the only major-league team in history to win five World Series in a row (1949–1953) and the only squad to win four consecutive batting titles (1936–1939).

The Yankees' story is not only loaded with successful seasons, it is also filled with superstars, some of the best-known players in the game's history. Babe Ruth was perhaps the greatest power hitter of all time; Lou Gehrig was one of the most durable athletes in the history of American sports; and Joe DiMaggio and Mickey Mantle were dynamic and multi-talented center fielders. Flamboyant slugger Reggie Jackson had an incredible sense of making the most of a big moment, and Don Mattingly was one of the most consistent hitters. Amazingly, these players represent only a small part of the many great talents who have played for New York.

Despite their glorious history, the Yankees were not successful during the early years of the franchise. The club became a member of the American League in 1903 and was then known as the "Highlanders." They were rarely high in the league standings, seldom finishing above fourth in the eight-team American League during the franchise's first 15 years. The team, which was also called the "Hilltoppers" and then finally the "Yankees" in 1913, was only the third-most popular club in New York City, behind the New York Giants and the Brooklyn Dodgers of the National League, which were much more successful. Finally, in 1918, tired of the Yankees being the "other" team in the Big Apple, the Yankees' owners persuaded Miller Huggins, the feisty manager of the St. Louis Cardinals, to accept a new position as manager of the New York Yankees team.

1 9 0 3

The Highlanders finished fourth in their first year in the AL under the guidance of manager Clark Griffith.

Hard-hitting first baseman Tino Martinez.

1 9 1 5

On April 15, pinstripes, now a Yankees tradition, first appeared on the club's uniforms.

Huggins decided to build his team on power hitting, and his first club, in 1919, led the American League with 45 home runs, mostly due to slugging outfielder Duffy Lewis. That same year, however, one player for the Boston Red Sox hit 29 homers all by himself. That player's name was George Herman Ruth, better known as "The Babe." Huggins begged Yankees owner Col. Jacob Ruppert to go after Ruth, and he did just that, purchasing the rights to Ruth from Boston and then offering him a contract with a salary four or five times larger than most major-league salaries at the time. Ruth, who began his career as a pitcher for the Red Sox but had become a full-time right fielder, joined the Yankees in time for the 1920 season.

Three years later, the Yankees, now among the top teams in baseball, added another slugger, a first baseman who would bat clean-up behind the amazing Ruth. The new man, a 6-foot, 200-pound power hitter from Columbia University in New York City, was named Lou Gehrig. Ruth and Gehrig were the major stars in a lineup that would eventually be known as "Murderers' Row." Behind the hitting of Ruth and Gehrig, the Yankees won four World Series titles and five American League pennants between 1923 and 1932. In all, Ruth played on seven pennant winners; Gehrig was a member of nine American League championship teams and eight World Series winners.

Ruth and Gehrig had a lot in common on the field—both were power hitters who had high batting averages—but they were as different as night and day off the diamond. Ruth was a playful sort, a little boy in a man's body; Gehrig, who had a more formal education than Ruth, was serious and reserved. The two superstars respected each other more than they liked each other.

Ruth was revered by the kids, and he was respected by his teammates, many of whom were in awe of his talents. Said Waite Hoyt, who was Ruth's teammate with the Yankees from 1921 to 1930, "To play on the same club with Ruth was not only a pleasure, it was a privilege—an experience which comes once in a lifetime. Babe was no ordinary man. He was superman to the ballplayers. Ballplayers who had played against him and who eventually joined the Yankees used to say, 'I knew how great he was when I played against him, but I never thought I'd see anything like this.' "

Ruth, who left the Yankees in the mid-1930s, retired with a .342 lifetime batting average. During his remarkable career he hit 714 regular-season home runs—and 15 homers during World Series play. Ruth topped the American League in home runs 12 times. In 1927, Ruth slammed 60 homers, a single-season record that stood until Roger Maris, another Yankee slugger, hit 61 in 1961. Ruth, perhaps the most feared power hitter of all time, managed to hit a home run about once every 12 times at bat. He was so famous that sportswriters began calling Yankee Stadium, into which the team moved during Ruth's early years with the club, the "House That Ruth Built."

If Ruth was spectacular, Gehrig was steady. Ruth was known for towering, tape-measure blasts; Gehrig was more of a line-drive hitter. "He could probably hit a ball harder in every direction than any man who ever played," said Yankee

1 9 2 3

Two historic events occurred on April 18: Yankee Stadium opened, and Babe Ruth hit the first home run there.

Early '80s slugger Reggie Jackson.

'80s pitcher Rich Gossage.

catcher Bill Dickey. "Lou could hit hard line drives past an outfielder the way I hit hard line drives past an infielder."

When Gehrig joined the Yankees in 1923, he initially sat on the bench. Veteran Wally Pipp was a standout at first base. Nevertheless, manager Miller Huggins was determined to use Gehrig somehow, and Huggins got his chance when Pipp complained of a headache June 1, 1925, and asked to be taken out of the lineup. Gehrig started at first base that day and remained there for 2,130 consecutive games, an all-time major-league record that stood until the Baltimore Orioles' Cal Ripken surpassed the mark in 1995. Today, nearly 75 years after Gehrig made his Yankees debut, sportswriters still refer to "Wally Pipp disease" any time a starter, in any sport, sits out a game or two and is replaced by a substitute who does well. Pipp's headache cost him any chance of ever regaining his starting spot with the Yankees.

Because Gehrig never came out of the lineup, most fans thought he was indestructible. In fact, Gehrig was given the nickname "Iron Horse" because of his durability. But he wasn't indestructible. By the beginning of the 1939 season, it was obvious that Gehrig wasn't himself. He was sluggish, and he couldn't seem to hit at all. What nobody knew at the time was that the mighty Gehrig was dying. Gehrig was diagnosed with an incurable disease known as amyotrophic lateral sclerosis, which destroys the nerve cells that control movement. Doctors told Gehrig there was no hope, but he refused to believe it. The illness forced him to retire during the 1939 season. On July 4 of that year, the Yankees held "Lou Gehrig Day" at Yankee Stadium. Before the game, an obviously weakened Gehrig walked slowly to the micro-

1 9 4 1

On June 2, at the age of 37, Yankees great Lou Gehrig, the man many thought was indestructible, died.

phone and, with the crowd's cheers almost drowning him out, said, "Today, I consider myself the luckiest man on the face of the earth." Two years later the Iron Horse was dead at the age of 37. Today, almost 60 years after his death, the illness that killed him is commonly referred to as "Lou Gehrig's Disease."

THE GREAT CENTER FIELDERS: DiMAGGIO AND MANTLE

1 9 4 6

Hall of Fame catcher Yogi Berra began his 18-year career with the Yankees club.

With both Ruth and Gehrig gone, the Yankees pinned their hopes on a dynamic young center fielder named Joe DiMaggio, a player who could hit homers and still have a high batting average. DiMaggio twice topped the American League in home runs—with 46 in 1937 and 39 in 1948—and won AL batting titles in 1939 and 1940. But DiMaggio is renowned for what he did in 1941, a year in which he didn't win any home-run or batting championships. It was the year Boston Red Sox slugger Ted Williams became the last hitter to average .400 in a season, but that year is still best known as the season DiMaggio recorded at least one base hit in 56 consecutive games. To give some perspective to "Joltin Joe's" feat, the next longest streak is 44 games. Of all the records set by Yankee players, Joe DiMaggio's 56-game streak may be the most remarkable.

"The 1941 streak was an unbelievable thing—day after day after day," said Yankees shortstop Phil Rizzuto. "I don't think he got a soft hit the entire 56 games. There were so many great games in the streak. He got up to 40 or 45, and you really couldn't see any difference in him. He just acted the same every day."

In his first full season as skipper, Casey Stengel led the Yankees to the World Series championship.

Success didn't affect DiMaggio; he seemed the same no matter what. "People didn't see DiMaggio like I did," said Yankees catcher Bill Dickey. "He just was never a guy who could let down in front of strangers. He was a guy who knew he was the greatest baseball player in America, and he was proud of it. He knew what the press and the fans and the kids expected of him, and he was always trying to live up to that image. That's why he couldn't be silly in public like I could, or ever be caught without his shirt buttoned or his shoes shined. He felt that obligation to the Yankees and to the public."

DiMaggio gave the Yankees 12 full seasons of flawless service. During his years in New York, the team won 11 pennants and 10 World Series titles. DiMaggio, who slammed 361 homers in his career, was named the American League Most Valuable Player three times—in 1939, 1941, and 1947. He compiled these lofty numbers despite missing three full seasons while serving in World War II. Despite his success, some of DiMaggio's teammates felt he didn't receive the credit he deserved. "I think DiMaggio was underestimated as a player," said Dickey. "He did things so easily, [that] people didn't realize how good he was. DiMaggio would hit a home run, but nobody would get excited. He could do so many things to keep the other team from beating you." DiMaggio conducted himself with such grace on and off the field that New York fans commonly referred to him as the "Yankee Clipper" after the elegant sailing vessels.

When DiMaggio retired after the 1951 season, Yankees fans wondered where the team would find someone to replace him. As it turned out, the Yankees didn't have to look

Like Mantle, Dave Winfield was a powerful hitter.

16   *Catcher Elston Howard starred for the Yanks in the 1950s.*

very far—only to right field, where a 20-year-old named Mickey Mantle was playing during DiMaggio's final season in New York. Mantle, who had grown up in Oklahoma, was unlike previous Yankees sluggers. A muscular switch-hitter, he could launch mammoth home runs either right- or left-handed.

Mantle had made an immediate impression on Yankees coaches the first time he took batting practice. Although he was only 18 years old at the time, he hit several balls that traveled more than 500 feet. Yankees manager Casey Stengel could hardly believe his eyes. "Tell ya how it is," Stengel said. "There are some who say he hits with more power right-handed, and there's others who say he hits with more power left-handed. They can't make up their minds. Now, wouldn't you say that was amazing? Personally, I hope they never find out."

Mantle, however, wasn't a star right away. He struggled at first in the big leagues and at one point called his father and told him he wanted to quit. Mantle's father showed up soon afterward and began packing the troubled youngster's bags. "I asked my dad what he was doing, and he looked at me real hard and said, 'I thought I raised you to be a man and not a quitter. I must be wrong, so let's go home.'" The young slugger convinced his Dad to let him try again, and almost immediately he began to terrorize American League pitching. The addition of the powerful Mantle made a great Yankees team into a dominant one. Such stars as pitchers Whitey Ford and Ralph Terry, shortstop Phil Rizzuto, second baseman Bobby Richardson, and catcher Yogi Berra already dotted the Yankee lineup. Rizzuto had been voted American

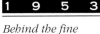

Behind the fine play of Mickey Mantle, the Yankees won their fifth consecutive world championship.

The next Yankee Hall-of-Famer, Rickey Henderson (pages 18-19).

1 9 6 1

Roger Maris' 61st home run broke Babe Ruth's single-season record for home runs.

League MVP in 1950, and Berra was the AL Most Valuable Player three times—in 1951, 1954, and 1955. By 1956, though, Mantle was New York's top player. In fact, he was probably the best player in all of baseball that year. Mantle won the Triple Crown in the American League in 1956 by leading the league in home runs (52), runs batted in (130), and batting average (.353). Not surprisingly, Mantle was voted the American League MVP.

Unfortunately for Mantle, who also won the league MVP honor in 1957 and 1962, his career was hampered by injuries, particularly to his knees. Once arguably the fastest player in the game, Mantle began to labor on his battered legs as early as the mid-50s. He still managed to retain some of his speed, but the pain took its toll. Mantle, though, played no matter how much his body ached. During the 1961 World Series against the Cincinnati Reds, Mantle was in the lineup despite an infection in his hip, which had developed while he had been hospitalized with a bad virus. The illness had come in a season when both Mantle and teammate Roger Maris were on pace to break Babe Ruth's single-season home-run record. Maris went on to break the record; Mantle went on to the hospital. He still managed to hit 54 home runs, second only to Maris's 61.

After missing the first two games of the series, Mantle played in games three and four, helping the Yankees to two victories and a 3–1 lead in the series. But he had to come out of the fourth game after hitting a single; the pain from the open wound on his hip was just too much. "It made me sick to look at the hole in his hip," said New York catcher Elston Howard. "It makes me sick to think about it. Nobody else would have played. Nobody. But Mickey isn't like normal people."

Despite Mantle's injury, the Yankees wound up winning the 1961 World Series in five games. A year later Mantle endured another series of injuries, but somehow managed to win league MVP honors and lead the team to another World Series triumph—this time over the San Francisco Giants. However, it would be the last World Series victory for the New York team for 15 years. The Yankees, behind the aging Mantle, won pennants in 1963 and 1964, but the team, and its star, soon fell off. By the late 1960s, the Yankees were no longer even pennant contenders. Mantle's body finally gave out, and he retired with 536 home runs, which remains the eighth-highest total in major-league history. There is no telling what Mantle might have achieved had he been healthy most of his career. As Casey Stengel said of Mantle, "He's the only man I ever saw who was a cripple and could outdo the world." Inducted into the Hall of Fame in 1974, Mantle died on August 13, 1995. A year later, a monument in his honor was unveiled in Yankee Stadium's Monument Park.

1 9 7 6

Don Gullett became the first free agent signed by the Yankees in the re-entry draft.

CONSISTENT HITTERS KEEP YANKS COMPETITIVE

The Yankees weren't outdoing many American League teams during the late 1960s and early 1970s. The club changed players, coaches, and managers, and nothing worked. Then in 1973, the Yankees had an ownership change that would bring about a brief reversal of the franchise's fortunes. Shipping magnate George Steinbrenner

New York's "Donnie Baseball," Don Mattingly.

bought the team and announced he would rebuild it into a champion, regardless of the cost. Steinbrenner then purchased such great talents as pitcher Jim "Catfish" Hunter and slugging outfielder Reggie Jackson. These players were combined with such Yankees stars as catcher Thurman Munson, third baseman Graig Nettles, first baseman Chris Chambliss, and relief pitcher Sparky Lyle to produce a rising power in the American League.

In 1976 the Yankees won the AL East and the pennant for the first time in 12 years, but were swept four games to none by the mighty Cincinnati Reds in the World Series. A year later though, nothing could stop the Yankees. They won the American League pennant and took a three-games-to-two lead against the Los Angeles Dodgers in the World Series. Then Jackson took over. Jackson, who had already slammed two homers in the series, hit homers on the first pitch in his first two at-bats of game six. When he came to the plate for the third time, the Yankee fans were on their feet screaming, "REG-GIE, REG-GIE, REG-GIE."

"I thought if I got a decent pitch, I could hit another one out," Jackson said. "Anyway, at that point, I couldn't lose. All I had to do was show up at the plate. They were going to cheer me even if I struck out. So the last [at-bat] was strictly dreamland." The last one was also a nightmare for the Dodgers, as Jackson hammered Charlie Hough's first offering over the center-field fence for his third home run of the game and fifth of the series. Only Babe Ruth had hit three homers in a World Series game; Jackson set a record for most home runs in a series. Behind Jackson's power, the Yankees won the game and the series.

On August 4, the Yankees held Phil Rizzuto Day and retired his uniform number 10.

Despite the loss of Dave Righetti, the Yankees and Don Mattingly were much improved.

Jackson and the Yankees won another World Series title in 1978, beating the Dodgers again. Pitcher Ron Guidry won the American League Cy Young Award, and shortstop Bucky Dent was the Most Valuable Player in the World Series. The Yankees also won the East Division of the American League in both 1980 and 1981, and were AL pennant winners in 1981. But then the success ended; the team's stars had gotten old, and Steinbrenner wasn't having too much luck replacing them with high-priced free agents. Still, both Dave Winfield and Rickey Henderson, a pair of outfielders, had several productive seasons for the club. And no Yankee was more consistent during the 1980s than first baseman Don Mattingly, who won the league batting title in 1984 and was the American League Most Valuable Player in 1985.

Mattingly brought an intense attitude to the ballpark every game. "Check Donnie's eyes during a game," said former Yankee pitcher Bob Tewksbury. "They're right out of a horror movie. He yells at opposing players. He paces in the dugout. I've never seen anyone compete with that kind of passion." Mattingly's intensity came naturally. "I don't actually dislike any opposing players, but I hate them when I play against them," Mattingly said. "Especially pitchers. I'm competing with them every at-bat, 162 games a season. You have to hate the guy. You have to get your mind into a sort of rage. I try to think of all the things the guy has done to irk me over the years."

Unfortunately for Mattingly, one of baseball's bright stars, the Yankees had forgotten how to be champions. From 1982 to 1994, the team did not win a title. "For a lot of clubs, 13 years without being in the postseason is no big deal," said Steinbrenner. "But for the New York Yankees, it is unacceptable." In 1994 the winning spirit was beginning to come back—the Yankees were in first place in August—but sadly, a players' strike cut the season short, and the playoffs were canceled. A frustrated Steinbrenner decided to reshape his team once again.

Right fielder Paul O'Neill became the seventh Yankee in history to lead the American League in hitting with his .359 average.

PLAYERS COME AND GO

At the end of the 1994 season, George Steinbrenner took a good look at his team. Center fielder Bernie Williams, who had joined the team in 1991, was a confident player with all the tools to be the next great Yankees center fielder. Right fielder Paul O'Neill provided run production and a high average with his smooth hitting stroke, and veteran third baseman Wade Boggs gave the Yanks a very steady bat and glove. With Mattingly still in top form, Steinbrenner had the building blocks for a great team, but more help was needed.

To complete his team, Steinbrenner added star pitcher David Cone through free agency and brought up young left-hander Andy Pettitte from the minor leagues. The overhauled team had to quickly form a winning chemistry, and fortunately they did. The Yankees made it back to the playoffs—but just barely. They finished second in the AL East, good enough to be the league's first-ever wild-card team.

New York would face the Seattle Mariners in the first round, and after five hard-fought battles, the Yankees were eliminated three games to two. The season was over, but

Dominant starting pitcher David Cone (pages 26-27).

Steinbrenner had seen that his team was close to championship caliber—it just needed a few more changes.

First, he hired Joe Torre to manage the team. A native of Brooklyn, New York, the calm, experienced Torre was a natural choice to handle the stresses of managing in the big-city pressure cooker. One of Torre's first moves was to insert rookie shortstop Derek Jeter into the starting lineup. "The kid's ready," noted a confident Torre. "It's time for him to earn his keep."

However, just as the season was about to begin, the Yankees were dealt a damaging blow. Don Mattingly announced he wanted to spend more time with his family and would not join the team. Mattingly would later finalize his retirement, and the Yankees would honor him by retiring his number (23) before the 1997 season. "Not having Donny here is awfully tough," said Boggs. "He's been the leader here for a long time, and we'll miss him; but we've got work to do, and it's time to get started."

1 9 9 5

Joe Torre was named the Yankee's 31st manager, replacing Buck Showalter November 2.

YANKEES RETURN TO GREATNESS

Opening Day 1996 was snowed out, so the Yankees had to wait until April 2 to start the season. But for the team's fans, the wait was worth it, as Derek Jeter's homer and clutch over-the-shoulder catch sparked the Yanks to a 7–1 win over the Cleveland Indians.

David Cone, the starting pitcher, was proud of his team. "Right now," he said, "we're searching for our own identity. We're trying to figure out how good we can be."

The good feelings of that first game continued. By midseason the team was in first place. Although the Yankees were not a great hitting team, their pitching was awesome. Cone, Andy Pettitte, free-agent addition Dwight Gooden, and closer Mariano Rivera seemed unstoppable.

By the end of the season, the Yankees had captured the AL East. After eliminating the Texas Rangers in the first round of the playoffs, New York faced the Baltimore Orioles for the AL championship and won four games to one. Next up would be the World Series against the defending champion Atlanta Braves.

1 9 9 6

Left-handed starter Andy Pettitte posted a 21–8 record with 162 strikeouts to lead the team.

The Yankees lost the first two games of the series but stormed back to win the next four. For the first time since 1978, the Yankees were world champions. The team with new players, mediocre hitting, and an unbelievable bullpen had done it. To celebrate their victory, the players ran laps around the field as fans chanted and yelled. "I've never heard that much noise," said Paul O'Neill afterward. "I thought the ground was shaking."

There was even more to celebrate when Torre was named American League Co-Manager of the Year (with Johnny Oates of the Texas Rangers). "It really is dreamlike," he said. "You wish everybody could experience this sometime in their life. It's very emotional."

One of the great stories of the 1996 season was the impressive play of Jeter. He hit .314 with 10 home runs and 78 RBIs. At one point in the season, he had a 17-game hitting streak. After the All-Star break, he evolved into one of the team's premier players.

"We had a lot of guys who were valuable," said Torre of Jeter. "I don't think we had one guy, player-wise, who

Current center-field star, Bernie Williams.

Steady veteran, outfielder Tim Raines.

was more valuable than him." In honor of his incredible first season in the majors, Jeter was named the AL Rookie of the Year.

1 9 9 8

The Yankees added more firepower to their lineup by acquiring All-Star second baseman Chuck Knoblauch from Minnesota.

THE GOOD FEELINGS CONTINUE

As the team began the next season, the players adjusted to their new status as champions and wondered if they could repeat their 1996 success. David Cone was healthy again after having an operation for an aneurysm in his pitching arm, and the team still had Bernie Williams and overwhelming closer Mariano Rivera on board. Derek Jeter was more experienced, as was pitcher Andy Pettitte.

However, the 1997 Yankees were not able to repeat as world champions. The team did win 96 games—good enough to capture the AL wild-card spot—but were eventually eliminated by the Cleveland Indians three games to two in the first round of the playoffs. Although the early knockout was disappointing, the pain has quickly turned to optimism for the future.

Early in the 1998 season, pitcher David Wells added to the Yankees' glorious history by throwing a perfect game against Minnesota on May 17. It was only the 13th perfect game in major league history. With stars like Jeter, Williams, Cone, O'Neill, slugging first baseman Tino Martinez, and former Rookie of the Year and 1997 second base Gold Glover Chuck Knoblauch in place to support the club's strong pitching, the Yankees can look forward to being regular visitors to the postseason for years to come.